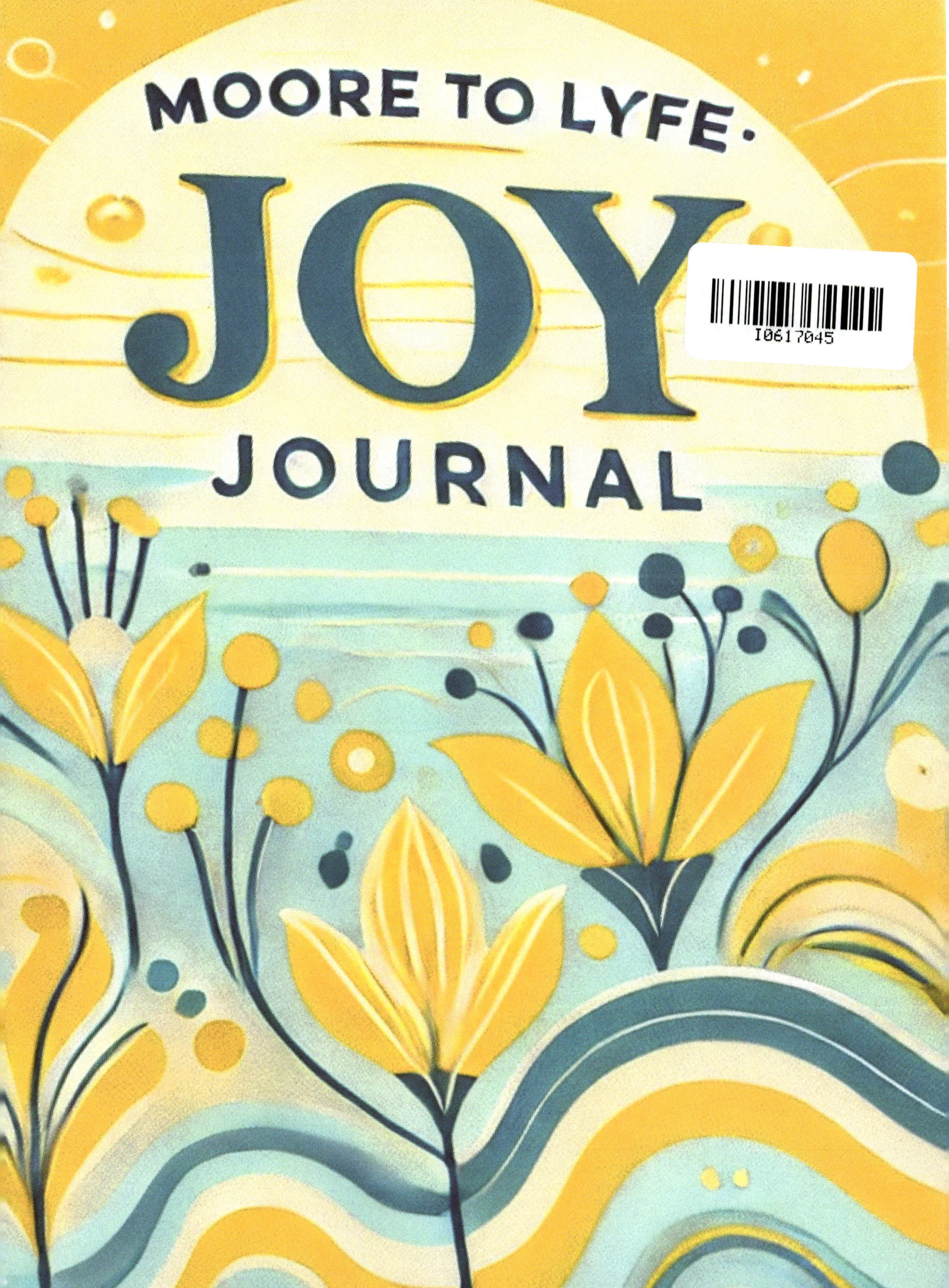

MOORE TO LYFE·

JOY

JOURNAL

Welcome

This journal is a tool for embracing and cultivating the joy that lies within you. Through daily reflections, prompts, and space for your thoughts, you'll be guided on a journey to find happiness, gratitude, and peace in the small moments of life. This journal is designed to help you process your thoughts, celebrate victories, and document the beauty of your

What to Expect:

- Daily Prompts: Simple questions to help you reflect on your day, focusing on positivity and personal growth.
- Affirmations: Uplifting statements to inspire and encourage you as you move through each day.
- Gratitude Space: A dedicated space for you to write down what you're thankful for, fostering a mindset of abundance.

How to Get the Most Out of Your Journal:

- Consistency is Key: Set aside a few minutes each day to write, allowing you to focus on your personal growth.
- Be Honest: Use this space to be real with yourself and embrace your journey, no matter where you are in it.
- Celebrate Your Progress: Track your growth over time, noting the moments that bring you joy and the lessons you've learned.

This journal is not just for writing; it's a space for healing, inspirations, and transformation. Each section invites you to reflect, discover, and celebrate moments of joy. Feel free to write, doodle, create, and breathe life into your personal story. Allow this journal to be a reminder that even in the most challenging times, there is always Moore to Lyfe. Take a leap into positivity, self-discovery, and joy!

Thank You

Hi there, and welcome!

I'm so glad you're here. Creating this Joy Journal came from a place deep in my heart — the same place that inspired Moore to Lyfe. "The journey you've just started is part of a bigger story. If you're looking for more inspiration and real-life stories of growth, check out Moore to Lyfe by Tamika Ford. It's a journey of its own that mirrors the power of transformation you're embracing here."

Just like the story in my book, life has shown me that even through the toughest moments, there's always light waiting to break through. Sometimes, we just need a little help finding it.

That's where this journal comes in. Life can be heavy — we carry so much: stress, uncertainty, and the weight of past experiences. But even in the middle of it all, joy is still there. It's in the quiet moments, the small victories, the belly laughs, and the peace that comes from knowing you're not alone.

This journal is your space to discover that joy — to pause, reflect, and remind yourself that no matter what life throws your way, you are still worthy of happiness. Just like the journey in Moore to Lyfe, this is about finding strength, healing, and the courage to keep going.

So take a deep breath, grab your favorite pen, and let yourself be honest here. There's no right or wrong way to do this — just show up for yourself. Joy is already within you; this journal is simply here to help you uncover it.

Your journey to more joy starts now. I'm honored to walk this path with you.

With love and light,

Tamika Ford

_____

Tamika Ford

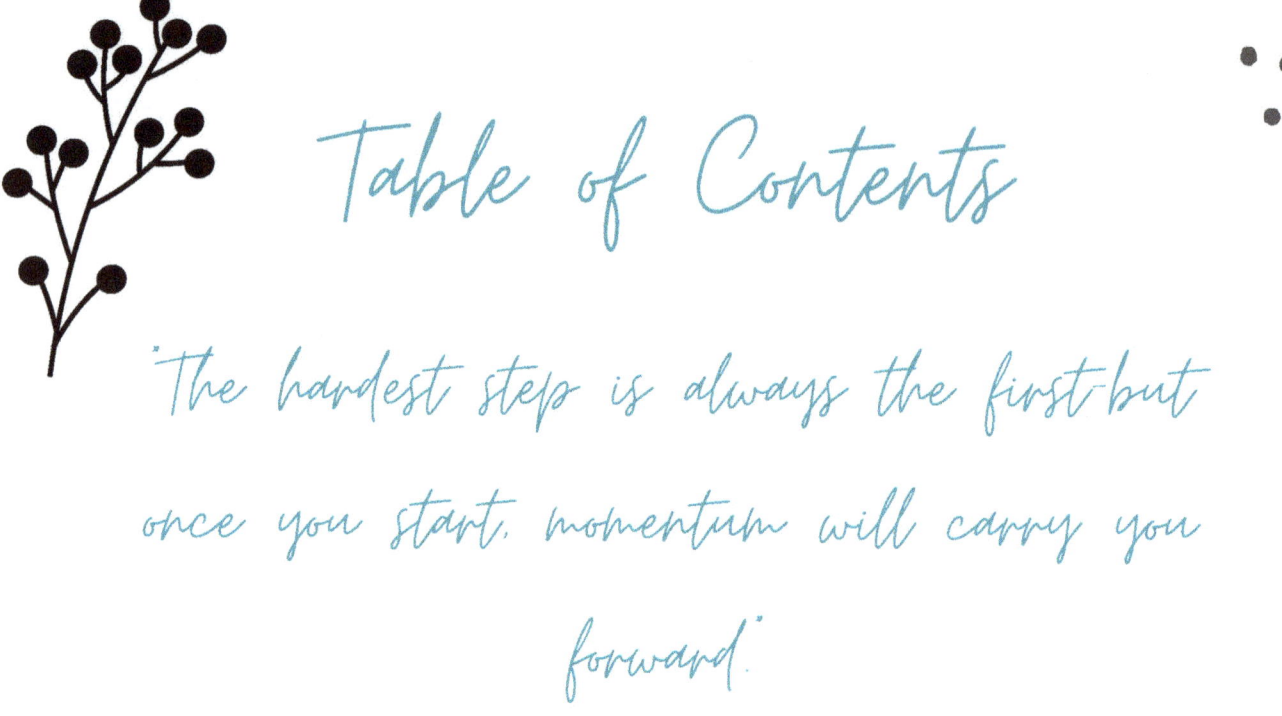

Table of Contents

"The hardest step is always the first but once you start, momentum will carry you forward."

Welcome to Your 30 Day Joy Journal

"Your Path to Healing, Happiness, and Living Your Best Life"

Each day will follow a pattern that helps you engage with your thoughts, celebrate wins, and set a positive tone for the day.

Each page will include:

Daily Affirmation: An inspiring quote or phrase to start the day.
Today's Highlights: Space to write three highlights from your day.
Gratitude Moment: A reminder to list one thing you're grateful for.
Reflection & Motivation: A short question to reflect positive thinking.
Joyful Action: A small action or activity to infuse joy into your day

Day 1

Daily Affirmation:
"I am enough, exactly as I am."

Today's Highlights:
1.
2.
3.

Gratitude Moment:
Today, I am grateful for...

Reflection & Motivation:
What brings you peace when life feels overwhelming?

Joyful Action:
 Take a 10-minute walk outside
and notice the sounds around
you.

Notes

Date: _____

_____

_____

_____

_____

_____

_____

_____

_____

_____

_____

_____

_____

_____

_____

Day 2

Daily Affirmation:
"I am in control of my happiness."

Today's Highlights:

1.
2.
3.

Gratitude Moment:

Today, I am grateful for...

Reflection & Motivation:

What is one small thing you can do today to make yourself smile?

Joyful Action:

 Dance to your favorite song for at least 3 minutes.

Notes

Date: _____

_____

_____

_____

_____

_____

_____

_____

_____

_____

_____

_____

_____

_____

_____

_____

_____

Day 3

Daily Affirmation:
"I have the power to create the life I want."

Today's Highlights:

1.

2.

3.

Gratitude Moment:

Today, I am grateful for...

Reflection & Motivation:

What's one thing you love about yourself?

Joyful Action:

❤️ Try a new recipe or make
your favorite meal.

Notes

Date: _____

_____

_____

_____

_____

_____

_____

_____

_____

_____

_____

_____

_____

_____

_____

Day 4

Daily Affirmation:

"I am open to the joy and abundance around me."

Today's Highlights:

1.
2.
3.

Gratitude Moment:

Today, I am grateful for...

Reflection & Motivation:

What's one thing that made you laugh today?

Joyful Action:

 Call or text a friend to say hi

Notes

Date: _____

Day 5

Daily Affirmation:
"I am worthy of love and happiness."

Today's Highlights:
1.
2.
3.

Gratitude Moment:
Today, I am grateful for...

Reflection & Motivation:
What's one thing you've overcome that made you stronger?

Joyful Action:
❤️ Treat yourself to a small gift or your favorite snack.

Notes

Date: _____

Day 6

Daily Affirmation: "I choose peace over worry."

Today's Highlights:

1.

2.

3.

Gratitude Moment:

Today, I am grateful for...

Reflection & Motivation:

What's one positive lesson you've learned recently?

Joyful Action:

 Take 5 deep breaths and center yourself.

Notes

Date: _____

_____

_____

_____

_____

_____

_____

_____

_____

_____

_____

_____

_____

_____

_____

Day 7

Daily Affirmation:
"I am capable of achieving greatness."

Today's Highlights:
1.
2.
3.

Gratitude Moment:
Today, I am grateful for...

Reflection & Motivation:
What's one goal you'd like to accomplish this week?

Joyful Action:
 Write down three
things you're proud of.

Notes

Date: _____

Day 8

Daily Affirmation:
"I am resilient and full of strength."

Today's Highlights:
1.
2.
3.

Gratitude Moment:
Today, I am grateful for...

Reflection & Motivation:

What's one time you turned a setback into a win?

Joyful Action:
💖 Spend 10 minutes stretching
or doing light yoga.

Notes

Date: _____

_____

_____

_____

_____

_____

_____

_____

_____

_____

_____

_____

_____

_____

_____

Day 9

Daily Affirmation:
"I trust that I am on the right path."

Today's Highlights:
1.
2.
3.

Gratitude Moment:
Today, I am grateful for...

Reflection & Motivation:
What's one way you've grown in the past year?

Joyful Action:
♥ Watch a funny video
or comedy show.

Notes

Date: _____

_____

_____

_____

_____

_____

_____

_____

_____

_____

_____

_____

_____

_____

_____

_____

Day 10

Daily Affirmation:
"I am grateful for the life I have."

Today's Highlights:

1.

2.

3.

Gratitude Moment:

Today, I am grateful for...

Reflection & Motivation:

What's one thing you appreciate about your body?

Joyful Action:

 Write yourself a kind note.
Stick on your bathroom mirror.
Repeat it DAILY!

Notes

Date: _____

_____

_____

_____

_____

_____

_____

_____

_____

_____

_____

_____

_____

_____

_____

_____

_____

Day 11

Daily Affirmation:
"I am exactly where I need to be."

Today's Highlights:
1.
2.
3.

Gratitude Moment:
Today, I am grateful for...

Reflection & Motivation:
What's one thing you've let go of that has brought you peace?

Joyful Action:
❤️ Go for a walk and
focus on your breathing.

Notes

Date: _____

_____

_____

_____

_____

_____

_____

_____

_____

_____

_____

_____

_____

_____

Day 12

Daily Affirmation:
"I am surrounded by love and support."

Today's Highlights:

1.

2.

3.

Gratitude Moment:

Today, I am grateful for...

Reflection & Motivation:

Who is someone that always makes you feel loved?

Joyful Action:

 Reach out and
thank them.

Notes

Date: _____

_____

_____

_____

_____

_____

_____

_____

_____

_____

_____

_____

_____

_____

_____

_____

Day 13

Daily Affirmation:
"I have the strength to face anything."

Today's Highlights:
1.
2.
3.

Gratitude Moment:

Today, I am grateful for...

Reflection & Motivation:

What's one way you can show yourself love today?

Joyful Action:

 Treat yourself to a cozy
evening with a book or movie.

Notes

Date: _____

Day 14

Daily Affirmation:
"I am proud of who I am becoming."

Today's Highlights:
1.
2.
3.

Gratitude Moment:
Today, I am grateful for...

Reflection & Motivation:
What's one thing you're excited about this month?

Joyful Action:
 Write down your
biggest dream.

Notes

Date: _____

_____

_____

_____

_____

_____

_____

_____

_____

_____

_____

_____

_____

_____

_____

_____

Day 15

Daily Affirmation: "I am worthy of all good things."

Today's Highlights:

1.
2.
3.

Gratitude Moment:

Today, I am grateful for...

Reflection & Motivation:

What's one thing you've done recently that made you feel proud?

Joyful Action:

 Buy yourself fresh flowers
or something small that makes
you smile.

Notes

Date: _____

Day 16

Daily Affirmation:
"I am becoming the best version of myself."

Today's Highlights:

1.
2.
3.

Gratitude Moment:
Today, I am grateful for...

Reflection & Motivation:
What's one skill or talent you'd like to develop further?

Joyful Action:

💖 Try a new hobby or revisit an old one

Notes

Date: _____

_____

_____

_____

_____

_____

_____

_____

_____

_____

_____

_____

_____

_____

_____

Day 17

Daily Affirmation:

"I choose to see the good in every situation."

Today's Highlights:
1.
2.
3.

Gratitude Moment:

Today, I am grateful for...

Reflection & Motivation:

What's one challenge you've faced that turned into a blessing?

Joyful Action:

 Write a list of five things that make you happy.

Notes

Date: _____

_____

_____

_____

_____

_____

_____

_____

_____

_____

_____

_____

_____

_____

Day 18

Daily Affirmation:
"I am attracting positivity and joy into my life."

Today's Highlights:
1.
2.
3.

Gratitude Moment:
Today, I am grateful for...

Reflection & Motivation:
What's one positive habit you'd like to strengthen?

Joyful Action:
 Watch a sunrise or sunset.

Notes

Date: _____

_____

_____

_____

_____

_____

_____

_____

_____

_____

_____

_____

_____

_____

_____

Day 19

Daily Affirmation: "I am stronger than my fears."

Today's Highlights:
1.
2.
3.

Gratitude Moment:
Today, I am grateful for...

Reflection & Motivation:

What's one fear you've overcome?

Joyful Action:
 Try something outside
of your comfort zone.

Notes

Date: _____

_____

_____

_____

_____

_____

_____

_____

_____

_____

_____

_____

_____

_____

_____

Day 20

Daily Affirmation:
"I radiate confidence and positivity."

Today's Highlights:
1.
2.
3.

Gratitude Moment:
Today, I am grateful for...

Reflection & Motivation:
What's one way you've inspired someone else?

Joyful Action:
💖 Compliment someone today.

Notes

Date: _____

_____

_____

_____

_____

_____

_____

_____

_____

_____

_____

_____

_____

_____

_____

Day 21

Daily Affirmation: "I am at peace with where I am."

Today's Highlights:
1.
2.
3.

Gratitude Moment:
Today, I am grateful for...

Reflection & Motivation:
What's one area of your life where you feel peace?

Joyful Action:
💖 Spend 10 minutes meditating
or sitting quietly.

Notes

Date: _____

_____

_____

_____

_____

_____

_____

_____

_____

_____

_____

_____

_____

_____

_____

_____

Day 22

Daily Affirmation: "I trust the timing of my life."

Today's Highlights:
1.
2.
3.

Gratitude Moment:

Today, I am grateful for...

Reflection & Motivation:

What's one sign that you're on the right path?

Joyful Action:
💗 Create a vision board or write down your dreams.

Notes

Date: _____

_____
_____
_____
_____
_____
_____
_____
_____
_____
_____
_____
_____
_____
_____
_____

Day 23

Daily Affirmation: "I am open to new experiences."

Today's Highlights:
1.
2.
3.

Gratitude Moment:

Today, I am grateful for...

Reflection & Motivation:

What's one new thing you'd like to try this year?

Joyful Action:
💗 Try a new food
or restaurant.

Notes

Date: _____

_____

_____

_____

_____

_____

_____

_____

_____

_____

_____

_____

_____

_____

_____

Day 24

Daily Affirmation:

"I am surrounded by peace and joy."

Today's Highlights:

1.

2.

3.

Gratitude Moment:

Today, I am grateful for...

Reflection & Motivation:

What's one place where you feel the most peaceful?

Joyful Action:

 Spend time in nature today.

Notes

Date: _____

_____

_____

_____

_____

_____

_____

_____

_____

_____

_____

_____

_____

_____

_____

_____

Day 25

Daily Affirmation:

"I am aligned with my purpose."

Today's Highlights:
1.
2.
3.

Gratitude Moment:

Today, I am grateful for...

Reflection & Motivation:

What's one thing that makes you feel fulfilled?

Joyful Action:  Write down your life's mission in one sentence.

Notes

Date: _____

_____

_____

_____

_____

_____

_____

_____

_____

_____

_____

_____

_____

_____

_____

_____

Day 26

Daily Affirmation:
"I am grateful for all that I have."

Today's Highlights:
1.
2.
3.

Gratitude Moment:
Today, I am grateful for...

Reflection & Motivation:
What's one way you can give back to others?

Joyful Action:
💖 Perform a random act of kindness.

Notes

Date: _____

_____

_____

_____

_____

_____

_____

_____

_____

_____

_____

_____

_____

_____

_____

_____

Day 27

Daily Affirmation:
"I am a beacon of light and hope."

Today's Highlights:
1.
2.
3.

Gratitude Moment:
Today, I am grateful for...

Reflection & Motivation:
What's one way you can spread positivity today?

Joyful Action:
 Send a thoughtful text to a loved one.

Notes

Date: _____

_____

_____

_____

_____

_____

_____

_____

_____

_____

_____

_____

_____

_____

_____

Day 28

Daily Affirmation:
"I am open to receiving love and joy."

Today's Highlights:
1.
2.
3.

Gratitude Moment:
Today, I am grateful for...

Reflection & Motivation:
What's one way you can show yourself more love?

Joyful Action:
 Take yourself on
a "date" (coffee,
movie, or treat).

Notes

Date: _____

Day 29

Daily Affirmation: "I am creating a joyful life."

Today's Highlights:

1.

2.

3.

Gratitude Moment:

Today, I am grateful for...

Reflection & Motivation:

What's one joyful memory you hold onto?

Joyful Action:
 Look through old photos and smile at the memories.

Notes

Date: _____

_____

_____

_____

_____

_____

_____

_____

_____

_____

_____

_____

_____

_____

_____

Day 30

Daily Affirmation:
"I am proud of how far I've come."

Today's Highlights:
1.
2.
3.

Gratitude Moment:
Today, I am grateful for...

Reflection & Motivation:
What's one thing you've learned about yourself this month?

Joyful Action:
 ❤️ Celebrate yourself - you've made it through 30 days!

Notes

Date: _____

_____

_____

_____

_____

_____

_____

_____

_____

_____

_____

_____

_____

_____

_____

✦ Congratulations ✦

On completing your 30-day journey! Keep the joy going!

You've successfully completed 30 days of affirmations! Your commitment to cultivating joy and success is truly inspiring. Remember, transformation comes with consistency-so feel free to revisit this journal daily or start a new one to continue your journey.
Like the author of Moore to Lyfe, there is always Moore joy to discover! Thank you for investing in yourself-may your life continue to overflow with happiness and success.
With gratitude,

Tamika Ford

BONUS

30 Days of Affirmations for Moore Joy
<u>Say them daily with confidence!</u>

✨ Week 1: Building a Positive Mindset

1 I am worthy of success and happiness.

2 I attract positivity and joy into my life.

3 My thoughts create my reality, and I choose uplifting ones.

4 Every day, I grow stronger, wiser, and more confident.

5 I release fear and welcome new opportunities.

6 Challenges are stepping stones to my success.

7 I deserve to live a fulfilling and joyful life.

🚀 Week 2: Confidence & Motivation

8 I trust myself to make the right decisions.

9 I am resilient, capable, and unstoppable.

10 My potential is limitless, and I embrace it fully.
I am becoming the best version of myself every day.

2 My energy is vibrant, and my motivation is unstoppable.

3 I am confident in my talents and skills.

4 I boldly step outside my comfort zone to achieve greatness.

Bonus

30 Days of Affirmations for Moore Joy

Say them daily with confidence!

💖 **Week 3: Emotional Strength & Gratitude**

15 I choose to focus on what brings me joy.

16 I am grateful for all the abundance in my life.

17 I radiate love, kindness, and positivity.

18 My past does not define me-I create my future.

19 I release negativity and welcome peace.

20 I am in control of my emotions and reactions.

21 Joy is my natural state, and I embrace it fully.

🏆 **Week 4: Success & Manifestation**

22 I attract success and wealth effortlessly.

23 Everything I desire is already on its way to me.

24 My hard work and dedication bring incredible rewards.

25 I am open to receiving abundance in all forms.

26 I take action toward my dreams every day.

27 Success flows to me with ease and grace.

28 I am aligned with my purpose and passion.

29 My life is filled with limitless possibilities.

30 I am creating a life I truly love and deserve.

✨ **Bonus Tip: Write or say these affirmations each morning to start your day with positive energy and focus!**

 *Self Note*

Date: _____

This section can be a safe space for letters of love, compassion, and self-encouragement.

"Write a letter to your future self. What do you envision for them, and what strength do you hope they carry?"

_____

_____

_____

_____

_____

_____

_____

_____

_____

_____

_____

_____

_____

_____

_____

_____

✦ Congratulations ✦

On completing your 30-day journey! Keep the joy going!

You've successfully completed 30 days of affirmations! Your commitment to cultivating joy and success is truly inspiring. Remember, transformation comes with consistency-so feel free to revisit this journal daily or start a new one to continue your journey.

Like the author of Moore to Lyfe, there is always Moore joy to discover! Thank you for investing in yourself-may your life continue to overflow with happiness and success.

With gratitude,

Tamika Ford

Benefits of 30 Days of Affirmations

Practicing 30 days of positive affirmations can have powerful effects on your mental, physical, and emotional well-being, ultimately leading to greater success and joy. Here's how:

🧠 Mental Benefits:

Strengthens positive thinking by rewiring the brain.
Boosts confidence and replaces self-doubt.
Reduces stress and anxiety by shifting focus.
Enhances clarity and decision-making.
Builds resilience, turning challenges into growth.

💪 Physical Benefits:

Lowers stress hormones, improving overall health.
Promotes better sleep and relaxation.
Increases energy and motivation.
Strengthens the immune system.
Encourages healthier habits and self-care.

💖 Emotional Benefits:

Cultivates joy, gratitude, and inner peace.
Improves relationships through self-acceptance.
Reduces negative self-talk and emotional distress.
Enhances emotional intelligence for better coping.
Creates a success-driven mindset.

🌟 How This Leads to Success & Joy:

A positive mind leads to better decisions, more energy, and greater resilience. With self-belief and emotional balance, success and joy become natural results of your daily practice!

You have made it to the end of the journal, now you'll be guided to look back over your entries and see the transformation. This is where you reflect on how your journey has shaped you and the new layers of joy you've uncovered along the way. You'll also have space to write about your next steps and how you plan to continue living your joy-filled life.. remember that growth is not always linear.

Just like in Moore to Lyfe, life will test you-but it will also reveal your strength. Take your time with each question. Allow yourself to feel the emotions that come up without judgment.

You are not defined by your setbacks- you are defined by your resilience.

1.   Every word you write is a step toward clarity, peace, and success. Keep going. "Just like in Moore to Lyfe, there's always Moore joy to add to your life. Continue growing and living the life you deserve!" 💙

Date.

Date.

Date.

Date.

Date.